Original title:
The Point of Life? It's a Work in Progress

Copyright © 2025 Creative Arts Management OÜ
All rights reserved.

Author: Rosalie Bradford
ISBN HARDBACK: 978-1-80566-293-8
ISBN PAPERBACK: 978-1-80566-588-5

The Evolution of a Questing Spirit

I started out with grand designs,
Chasing dreams like overcooked fries.
But here I am with mismatched socks,
Navigating life like it's a paradox.

I built a castle from cardboard boxes,
Adding glitter, but losing my choices.
Each step feels like a dance slightly wrong,
Yet I find the rhythm in a silly song.

I ponder deeply, or not at all,
Like a cat that's caught at a wall.
I leap, I trip, but hey, I laugh,
Sketching my journey like a funny giraffe.

In the end, it's about the ride,
With rubber chickens right by my side.
So here's to quests that twist and turn,
And all the lessons we get to learn.

Rainbows Born from Life's Storms

When life gives you lemons, make grape juice,
And watch as folks wonder, 'What's the good excuse?'
Chaos reigns in colorful hues,
As rain clouds dance and drop their blues.

With umbrellas turned inside out, I prance,
Splashing in puddles as the raindrops dance.
My hair looks like a dampened mop,
But that won't stop me; I'll never stop!

Through every storm, I hoot and jest,
Wearing mismatched shoes that I love the best.
With every thunderous, hearty laugh,
I sketch my path on life's crazy graph.

Oh, the surprises that life can serve!
Like a jigsaw puzzle that's lost its nerve.
So I dance in the rain, with a silly grin,
Embracing the chaos, where fun begins!

Ink on an Open Page

With scribbles wide and deep,
My thoughts take flight like sheep.
Some make sense, some make none,
But all of them are just for fun.

Inky fingers, stains galore,
My paper's hardly ever bore.
Every mark, a chance to laugh,
Life's a doodle, not a graph.

Unraveling the Threaded Knot

Life's a yarn, all tangled tight,
Pull a string, oh what a fright!
It twists and twirls like a dance,
Making sense? Not a chance!

Grab some scissors, cut it here,
Spin a tale, drink a beer.
For every snag, there's room to weave,
Embrace the mess, just believe!

A Symphony of Changes

Each note played in key or flat,
Sounds like life—a noisy chat.
Some days a solo, others a band,
Making music, not all planned.

In playful tones, we laugh and cry,
Forget the rules, just give it a try.
Life's a jam, unpredictable,
Dance like nobody's visible.

Horizons Yet to Explore

Maps are scribbled, plans askew,
But hey, that's what adventures do!
Who needs a route? We'll just wing,
Life's more fun when you don't cling.

From mountains high to valleys low,
We'll stumble, trip, but off we go!
Undefined paths, lost in delight,
With laughter as our guiding light.

Labyrinthine Hopes and Dreams Await

In a maze of whims and whirs,
Chasing dreams with wild flurs,
I trip on wishes, grasp at air,
My aspirations, quite a flare.

With each turn, a comic slip,
Life's a dance, a silly trip,
We laugh at paths that lead us wrong,
Yet find our joy in the absurd throng.

Mapping the Terrain of Inner Landscapes

Where thoughts collide like bumper cars,
I navigate with snacks and jars,
A map that's drawn in crayon bright,
Guiding me through the endless night.

Each twist could spark a chuckle loud,
As I weave through the pondering crowd,
Who knew a path could be this fun,
With laughs and snacks, we've almost won.

Currents of Change in a Still River

A river flows without a plan,
Yet fish still swim and ducks still tan,
Change comes gently, without a fuss,
My boat's afloat, it's quite a plus.

With each ripple, a giggle flows,
While I ponder all that life bestows,
Caught in currents, I wave hello,
To every thought, like shadows throw.

Pebbles in the Stream of Consciousness

I toss pebbles with glee and style,
In thoughts that wander a thousand miles,
Each splash is like a quirky thought,
Tickling the brain, a giggle caught.

In the stream where ideas tumble,
I trip on rocks but never grumble,
For every stone is a chance to play,
A merry dance on this wacky way.

Via Negativa: Finding Meaning in Absence

I'm on a quest, but where's my map?
I lost it somewhere, in a catnap.
Finding meaning in a missing sock,
Or in the silence of an empty clock.

Absence makes the heart grow fonder,
Why's it so hard to find that wonder?
Like socks that vanish in the wash,
I ponder meaning, then I just nosh.

In the fridge, leftovers seem to call,
Life's great mysteries behind the wall.
Maybe it's the crumbs that tell a tale,
Of lunch gone wrong, or laughter pale.

Yet here I sit with snack in hand,
Absurdity's lessons, so unplanned.
For meaning found in things now lost,
Can be quite funny, at no cost.

Tracing Lines of Fate and Choice

They say fate draws lines upon our face,
But mine looks like a curious lace.
Decisions made with a wink and grin,
Maps of chaos, where to begin?

Should I have chosen pizza or cake?
Both look so fine, for goodness' sake!
In choices vast, I often find,
The best ones come unplanned, unlined.

Paths are crossed like tangled shoelaces,
One wrong step leads to funny places.
Did I trip on fate or choose to fall?
The universe chuckles, it's all a ball.

Lines of fate twist, they turn and play,
Who said the journey has to be gray?
In scribbles of laughter, choices reflect,
Life's messy doodles, what did you expect?

Building Bridges Over Chasms of Fear

I've got a fear of heights, but here I stand,
Building bridges with a wobbly hand.
Two planks and a wish, can it hold me tight?
If I fall in the chasm, is it left or right?

With courage like jelly, I start to sway,
Next to a gopher, who's judging my play.
He laughs as I string my hopes on a line,
Telling me 'Dude, just add some design.'

Oh, the chasms are deep, and they mock my speed,
But giggles and glue are what I need.
I'll leap and I'll bound, I'll laugh as I fly,
For what's life without courage? Just do or die.

So here's to the bridges made out of fear,
Crafted with laughter, let's all persevere!
Each step a wobbly, hilarious cheer,
Come join me, my friend, on the bridge, let's steer!

The Rhythm of Rebirth and Renewal

In springtime blooms, a curious sprout,
It wiggles and giggles, leaps about.
With petals like laughter, colors in view,
Nature's funny dance, oh how it grew!

I tried to plant seeds of hopes and dreams,
But my thumb's a mishap, or so it seems.
Yet every time blooms a cheeky weed,
Renewal's rhythm dances in need.

Death, they say, is not the end,
It's just a fade, a quirky bend.
Like socks in the dryer, spinning around,
Out pops a fresh start, look what I've found!

Life's cycles are silly, just take a chance,
Each twist and turn, a goofy dance.
With laughing sprouts and joyful tunes,
Rebirth tickles under the moon!

Chasing Shadows of Tomorrow

In the mirror of my mind, I play,
Chasing dreams that dance away.
They giggle, twirl, and then they flee,
Like socks lost in the laundry sea.

I stretch for stars that fade at dawn,
As I start my day, I yawn and fawn.
With coffee cups and hopeful sighs,
I tiptoe past the small goodbyes.

The Constant Quest for Meaning

I ponder deep through lunchtime snacks,
Diving into life's little cracks.
Is it in the pie, or cake I see?
Or maybe it's just pizza for me.

I scribble notes on paper plates,
Seeking answers 'neath my dinner dates.
Philosophers would shake their heads,
While I recount meals in my threadbare threads.

Threads of Existence Woven Together

Life's a quilt of rags and tags,
Sewn with laughter, joy, and snags.
I stitch my days with silly threads,
And patch up dreams beneath my beds.

Each moment's a knot tied tight in space,
With weird designs that dance with grace.
Unruly patterns, mismatched style,
But hey, it's fashion—stay awhile!

The Unsung Symphony of Growth

Life's a symphony of squeaks and squawks,
Played by an orchestra of wise old clocks.
Each tick and tock a note of cheer,
As I march in tune, my piggy ears.

I trip on beats, I slip on rhymes,
Dancing my way through all the climes.
Who knew growth meant stepping wide?
With flair and flair, I take it in stride.

Chiseling Dreams from Solid Blocks

With a chisel and a grin, we try,
Our dreams carved from a rock, oh my!
Each whack's a laugh, a silly guess,
As we sculpt our lives with finesse.

A block of stone, a block of cheese,
We chip away with much more ease.
Sometimes it crumbles, sometimes it sings,
In our hands, it's just silly things.

Each little piece that flies away,
Is just another reason to play.
We giggle as the shavings fly,
Who knew a bump could make us cry?

So here we stand with tools anew,
Chiseling dreams, but what's the clue?
It's messy art, a constant chase,
At least there's laughter in this place.

The Path Not Taken: A Life Unwritten

I wandered down that winding path,
With two roads there, it gave me math.
One leads to chores, the other fun,
Yet somehow, both are on the run.

I chose the left, to take a break,
Found a cat who just won't wake.
We laughed so hard, I dropped my shoe,
And now I'm lost, but who knew?

With every step, I question more,
Was it that one? Or just a bore?
A little dance with life's surprise,
Unwritten tales in each disguise.

So here I skip through unturned stones,
Collecting moments, dreams, and bones.
Life's a script, no lines to rhyme,
We make it funny, one step at a time.

Glimmers of Truth in the Night Sky

Stars whisper secrets to those who dare,
To find the truth hiding everywhere.
But most just trip on their own shoes,
While chasing glimmers, they might lose.

The moon just rolls its eyes and grins,
While we argue about losses and wins.
"Look up!" it shouts, "just laugh tonight,
Life's bright when you're in delight!"

Clusters of pearls, like hiccups in space,
Remind us to giggle at life's weird pace.
For truth is often wrapped in jest,
And laughter's always what we like best.

So here we are, with stars to guide,
Waving at the cosmos, oh what a ride.
We dance with truth, let laughter fly,
In sparkling skies, we'll never die.

The Adventure of Living in Between (Moments)

In moments lost, where time slips by,
We juggle laughter and an awkward sigh.
Life's a circus with bits of flair,
As we tumble down without a care.

Caught in the waiting, a funny pause,
Like pasta cooking, without a cause.
Do I stir or do I wait?
The clock just laughs, I'm late, I'm late!

Between the chaos and calm delight,
I'll take a selfie with a blushing fright.
These moments matter, or maybe not,
Still, I'll brew coffee, give it a shot.

Adventure awaits in each weird twist,
Between the mundane and the blissed.
So let's embrace the in-between,
Life's funny stories are yet unseen.

Ink Runs Dry, Yet Inspiration Flows

When the pen gives up, takes a nap,
I scribble doodles, what a trap!
My thoughts may wobble, dance off track,
But humor helps me bounce right back.

Colors burst from an empty page,
A silly bear sets the stage.
With laughter's ink, I paint anew,
Life's messy, but it's fun to do!

My ideas tumble, roll, and flop,
Yet I keep scribbling, I won't stop.
Each slip and slide—a chance to play,
Creativity's here to stay!

So when my thoughts all seem to freeze,
I laugh at chaos, catch the breeze.
With ink on fingers, I'll always go,
For in this mess, my wild dreams flow!

The Puzzle of a Life Yet to Solve

Pieces scattered, oh what a sight,
A puzzle box that just won't bite.
Each time I fit one, two jump away,
It's a game I play day by day.

Corners are tricky, edges beguile,
I mix up the shapes with a big goofy smile.
Life's awkward jigsaw keeps me on my toes,
Even the flaws help the picture grow.

My cat jumps in, thinks it's all his,
Knocking pieces, he's full of fizz.
I toss him a treat, we share the fun,
Together we laugh, as we puzzle as one.

So if you lose track, don't you fret,
Embrace the chaos, and place your bet.
In the game of life, just play your part,
For every odd piece can be true art!

Rafting Through Rapids of Reflection

In a boat made of thoughts, I navigate,
Through whirlpools of worries, I contemplate.
Paddling hard, I start to smile,
What a wild ride, it's worth the while!

Each splash is laughter, bouncing way high,
As waves of wisdom make me sigh.
I bob and weave through fears galore,
Oh, look! There's my courage on the shore!

Ropes of doubt try to pull me back,
But I'm on a journey, no looking slack.
The rapids might chase, but I don't mind,
Every twist and turn, a gem to find.

So let the waters swirl and rush,
I'll ride the rapids with a gleeful hush.
Reflecting on moments, both big and small,
Each droplet a story— catch me if you can, y'all!

Forging Identity from the Ashes of Doubt

In the furnace of life, doubts do spark,
Out of the ashes, I leave my mark.
With a hammer of humor, I mold my fate,
Bending the metal, it's never too late.

Flames flicker, and sparks fly high,
A funny face in the coals nearby.
I chuckle at shadows that come to play,
For in this chaos, I find my way.

Each twist of the metal, a new design,
Doubts may linger, but that's just fine.
I'll forge my identity, giggle and grin,
With every crack, a new tale begins.

So let the fires burn and glow bright,
I'll wear my armor made of laughter and light.
From ashes to treasures, I boldly proclaim,
Life's a comedy show, and I'm glad I came!

Awaking to the Unfinished Story

I woke up today with a sock on my head,
Not sure where I am, or what lies ahead.
My coffee's gone cold, my toast is a flop,
But hey, it's a start, I won't hit the stop.

The calendar's filled with doodles and notes,
And memories vague as my old, rusty boats.
I scribble my dreams on the back of my hand,
With ink that will fade, but I still have a plan.

The cat's staring hard, as if reading my mind,
While I'm searching for answers I can't seem to find.
Life's like a puzzle with pieces all mixed,
I'm just here to giggle as the plot gets twisted.

So here's to the chaos, the mess that we make,
With laughter and love, there's no need to forsake.
I'll dance through the failures, I'll wear them with pride,
In this wild, unfinished, and joy-filled ride.

Notes from the Heart's Journey

In a world full of maps, I'm lost on my own,
I trip on my shoelaces, but hey, I have grown.
With a heart that keeps bouncing, like jelly on toast,
I find every failure deserves a good roast.

My emotions are scattered like leaves in the breeze,
I'll pick them all up, or just scatter with ease.
Is that joy I just felt, or was it a sneeze?
I guess both are valid, as life tries to tease.

I talk to the plants as they nod in reply,
With soil on my shirt, I don't even ask why.
They whisper their secrets while I sip on my tea,
"Just water us lightly, and always be free."

So here's to the heart, so messy yet sweet,
It's a rollercoaster ride under a comical sheet.
I'll write down my notes, in a notebook from 1985,
Because the journey's the joke, and I'm glad I'm alive.

Unveiling the Layers of Existence

Like peeling an onion, it gets quite intense,
Each layer reveals another bonus expense.
I laugh through the tears as they stream down my face,
Existence is funny, a peculiar race.

In the mirror, I see a wild, tangled hair,
A snapshot of mornings when I just didn't care.
Dressed in mismatched socks, I strut down the street,
With laughter my guide, I can't be discreet.

People with questions all want me to share,
But I'm busy retracing my steps in midair.
I'll juggle my dreams like a clown at a fair,
With laughter as currency, I've nothing to spare.

So here's to the layers, let's take them apart,
With a wink and a giggle, we play the right part.
Each layer we shed is a jest in disguise,
After all, life's a joke wearing marvelous ties.

The Fragility of Being in Motion

With each step I take, the ground feels unsteady,
I stumble through life like I've lost all my ready.
The sky gives me side-eyes, with clouds full of sass,
As I trip on my shoelaces, while running fast.

Life's like a ballet, but I'm more of a clown,
With pirouettes awkward, I spin and I frown.
Every fall is a dance, every laugh is a win,
In this tangled up journey, I'm learning to grin.

The clocks keep on ticking, and I've misplaced time,
While writing my saga in a notebook of rhyme.
With a tea cup as my stage and the world as my crew,
I'll tap dance on chaos, and give y'all a view.

So raise up a cheer for the slips and the trips,
With joy in our hearts and some light-hearted quips.
We'll moan and we'll joke as we glide through the fray,
In this precious, fragile, and silly ballet.

The Art of Becoming Each Day

Each morning starts with a coffee mess,
Pour it in, and hope for less stress.
The mirror reflects an artful sight,
A masterpiece, or a morning fright?

Socks that mismatch, a fashion trend,
Pajamas and dreams, my closest friends.
With laughter and grace, I try to improve,
Dancing through life, trying to groove.

Mistakes become my trusted pals,
I trip on hope, yet still stand tall.
Every stumble is a new chance,
To turn each mishap into a dance.

And as the sun sets with a wink,
I toast my heart with another drink.
Tomorrow's canvas is still unplanned,
Each brushstroke leads to where I stand.

Whispers of Hope in Hectic Days

Rushing through chaos, my mind's in a spin,
Hiccups of laughter, let the fun begin!
A calendar's filled, yet I'm on my way,
To find hidden treasures in the fray.

Coffee fuels dreams in this bustling game,
Where sanity's loose, and the mud's my name.
Behind every corner, wisdom does lurk,
In the smallest joys, life does its work.

Amid spilled papers and a tangled heart,
A giggle escapes, a fine work of art.
Each deadline met with a cheeky grin,
It's all very funny—let the day begin!

So, here's to the messes we make with flair,
In every wild moment, there's love to share.
With whispers of hope in the busy grind,
A laugh, a smile, and peace I find.

Sketches of a Soul Still Unfolding

A crayon in hand, I'm drawing with glee,
Not all my lines want to flow free.
With shades of regret and erasers nearby,
I tantrum with joy, oh me, oh my!

Chasing the sunset with glitter and stars,
In this art gallery filled with my scars.
Each sketch tells a tale, a jest, or a jibe,
In creating my life, I play with the vibe.

A dab of confusion, a splash of delight,
Whisked into laughter in the dim of the night.
What's next on the canvas? A coffee cup?
We'll paint over limits and fill it right up!

So here's to the colors I yet have to blend,
With plenty of humor around every bend.
Each stroke a reminder that I'm just begun,
In this sketch of a life? Oh, it's all in the fun!

Journeys of a Reluctant Wanderer

Packing my bags, I can barely see,
Where's the remote? Not lost, just me!
Stumbles abound as I wade through the fray,
But every wrong turn leads to more play.

The road signs giggle, and so do I,
"Visit the ocean!" my dreams flutter by.
With flip-flops on, I chase with a grin,
Dodging the waves, letting trouble swim.

Navigating life is an unmappped spree,
A comedy of errors; oh, can't you see?
Every pitfall just adds to the script,
In the theater of laughter, I'm fully equipped.

Stopping for snacks, the fun never ends,
These journeys, my dear, are where joy transcends.
So here's to the roads, both twisted and wide,
With nothing but laughter to be my guide.

The Canvas Unrolled

Life's a canvas, smudged and torn,
With paints we spill before the morn.
Doodles of dreams in colors bright,
Oh, what a mess, but what a sight!

We scribble hearts, we sketch some stars,
Draw mustaches on old cars.
Each stroke a giggle, a laugh, a cheer,
For art is better when we don't steer!

So let the paint fly, don't be shy,
It's not a masterpiece - just by and by.
Splashes of joy, blots of regrets,
A colorful life with no resets!

At the end, we'll see our clumsy flair,
A wacky mural, beyond compare.
In the gallery of life, take a glance,
It's the goofy strokes that give us a chance!

Tides of Reflection

The ocean waves wash in and out,
Just like my thoughts, no doubt.
One day I'm deep, the next I'm light,
Trying to swim, but sometimes I fight!

Reflection pools mirror a confused face,
Is it the tide or my place?
I wear flippers, yet trip on sand,
It's a splashy show, not quite as planned!

Seagulls squawk with a hint of sass,
While I ponder if I'll ever pass.
The tide comes in, and I splash around,
In this dance of growth, joy is found!

So here's to the waves and the sandy falls,
Life's a beach, even with its brawls.
I float, I dive, in laughter and cheer,
Just keep swimming, the shore is near!

Sculpting Time

With clay in hand, I shape my day,
A lumpy figure in disarray.
The arms go floppy, the head falls flat,
But hey, it's art, and I love that!

I chisel off my worries with glee,
Each chip a laugh, oh can't you see?
Time's a block, it shifts and bends,
Always creating, it never ends!

A masterpiece? Maybe not today,
But I'll keep sculpting in my quirky way.
Sometimes it's a bust, other days a gem,
Each piece a story, a little mayhem!

So grab your tools, let's whittle some fun,
In this workshop of life, we've only begun.
For every goof and every rhyme,
Is just another chance, sculpting time!

In Pursuit of Wholeness

I chase my dreams like a cat with yarn,
Tangled and fumbling, oh so far.
Every loop a laugh, every twist a tease,
In pursuit of wholeness, I'm just a tease!

I try to fit in like misplaced socks,
Bumping around like a box of blocks.
Searching for pieces that simply won't mesh,
But hey, misfits can still make a fresh!

In journeys quirky, I find my dance,
Each wobble and wiggle, a silly chance.
With a giggle here and a snicker there,
Life's collage of fun, beyond compare!

So let's embrace the puzzle's strange,
For wholeness is wild, and nothing can change.
We're all bits and parts in a comical flow,
Together we shine, together we glow!

Unfinished Tapestry

Threads are tangled, what a mess,
A quilt of dreams, in need of less.
Doodles scribbled on my fate,
I'm late to the show, but isn't it great?

Colors clash and patterns sway,
Trying hard to find my way.
Each stitch a giggle, a laugh, a sigh,
Who knew that life would be tried on the fly?

In the chaos, I find delight,
A patchwork quilt of sheer insight.
Knots undone, stories await,
This weaving's fun, I can't wait!

Maybe someday, it'll come together,
Like a puzzle piece, or sunny weather.
Until that day, I'll jest and grin,
For every flaw, I'll wear like skin.

Whispers of Tomorrow

Oh dear future, what's your game?
I'll be there, just don't be lame.
You whisper sweetly, then pull away,
Like a mirage in bright sunray.

I plan and scheme, it's all in fun,
But every plan declares it's done.
A cocktail mix of hope and doubt,
Each sip I take, I scream and shout.

Tomorrow's here, but what a tease,
With every promise, it likes to freeze.
I'll stand in line, with time to spare,
Waiting for laughs and absent flair.

So here's to you, my fickle friend,
May your whispers lead to the end.
I'll dance through days both lost and found,
In this funny game, life spins around.

Journey in Perpetual Motion

On this road of twists and turns,
I trip over lessons, bump my burns.
Each mile a journey, oh so grand,
With snacks and giggles, and coffee in hand.

Maps are great, but I lost mine,
Just wandering aimless, feeling divine.
I ask for directions, oh what a joke,
They send me off down a road of smoke.

Every stop a pause to think,
Of plans and hopes served on the brink.
Yet in the chaos, I find my pace,
Chasing the winds in a joyful race.

So let's applaud this wild delight,
For every misstep, there's laughter tonight.
This motion is endless, oh can't you see?
Life's a highway, come laugh with me!

Mosaic of Unfulfilled Dreams

Pieces scattered, bright as day,
Each one whispers, come out and play.
Painting visions on the go,
A splash of color, a touch of woe.

Dreamt of riches, but settled for fun,
In my heart, I keep a ton.
Every shard, a moment I've missed,
Caught in a whirlwind of hopeful twists.

Oh, I may not be the grand design,
But in this chaos, I still shine.
A mosaic made of giggles and sighs,
My masterpiece lives in the messy skies.

So let's celebrate what's out of reach,
Every folly teaches, oh what a breach.
In this art of life, I'll endlessly scheme,
For each flawed piece is a brand new dream.

Embrace of the Uncertain

In socks that clash, we strut our stuff,
With shaky steps, we laugh aloud.
Life's a circus, a big buffoon,
With each misstep, we wear our crown.

Juggling dreams like juggling fruit,
Most end up squashed, but we still cheer.
A dance with chaos, our favorite tune,
Together we waltz, fueled by good beer.

Plans made on paper, yet soggy by rain,
We snicker at fate, laughing all the way.
Maps that lead nowhere now hold some fame,
We claim our wrong turns in whimsical play.

So raise a glass to the wild unknown,
To blunders and antics, our love laid bare.
Life's not a straight line, it's a rom-com throne,
In the embrace of the uncertain, we dare!

Passageways to Possibility

Steps lead us forward, but oh what a mess,
Through doors that squeak and windows that shake.
We zig-zag around with garish finesse,
It's a treasure hunt, for our own sake!

With maps upside down, we wander and roam,
Finding gold in the mundane and meek.
Each corner a giggle, each turn is a poem,
Where lost socks meet laughter, so to speak.

Doors once forbidden swing wide with a bang,
Quirky passageways beckon our fate.
Tripping on marbles, we twirl, and we sang,
Creating our symphony, never too late.

Passageways open as we stumble through life,
With giggles that echo, joys wrapped in light.
Each odd little journey, each bump, every strife,
Is a colorful step in our dance of delight!

Seasons of the Soul

Spring brings the laughter, oh what a tease,
With blooming mischief and pollen-filled air.
We dance with the daisies, do as we please,
A joyride of whimsies, free as a hare.

Summer flares bright with sunburned smiles,
Barbecue blunders become summer's song.
We splash in the puddles, travel for miles,
While ice-cream drips down, it's where we belong.

Autumn walks in on a pumpkin parade,
With leaves that gossip and whisper their tales.
We trip over visions that memories made,
Collecting our quirks like colorful snails.

Winter's a quilt of misfit delight,
With cocoa spills marking our joyous spree.
We snuggle and chuckle, hearts warm through the night,
In seasons of soul, we're forever carefree!

The Craft of Existence

With glitter and glue, we stitch life's great quilt,
A patchwork of joy and the chaos we pen.
Each fabric a story, each mishap, a jilt,
But somehow it's mighty, this great mess we spin.

We craft our odd tools, each laugh a sharp chisel,
Sculpting our hopes from leftover dreams.
Carving the quirks with a wild little drizzle,
Our masterpiece sparkles, or so it seems.

Mistakes are the brushes, they color our fate,
With strokes that are silly, yet wonders they brew.
We dance through the mess, and we celebrate,
With art shared in giggles, heart paint flying too.

So here's to the craft, the quirky, the true,
To laughter and friendship, our bonds made so fine.
Life's canvas may wobble, but oh what a view,
In the craft of existence, we always combine!

The Colors of Reflection and Renewal

In a box of crayons, bright and bold,
I chose the one that never got old.
With smudged lines and colors that blend,
I painted my thoughts, a messy trend.

Like a jigsaw puzzle, missing some pieces,
My plans were good; fate had its releases.
With each new stroke, I'd giggle and cheer,
As the canvas of chaos became so clear.

Each splash of humor, a lesson to learn,
Dancing with colors, oh how they turn.
From blues of the past to yellows of glee,
For my messy little art is just so free.

So here's to the palette, the laughter, the fun,
This masterpiece isn't quite done.
With every mishap, giggles arise,
Life's greatest work is a sweet surprise.

Timelines Intersecting: A Life's Journey

I queued up in life's big amusement park,
Riding roller coasters that hit like a spark.
Each twist and turn, a sprinkle of fate,
I laughed with the loops — who could contemplate?

Bumped into my past, awkward and weird,
With time-traveling hiccups, oh, how I steered.
Dodgeball with moments that just won't stay still,
In this quirky journey, it's laughter I spill.

Maps in my pocket, the routes all out of whack,
But my compass points to joy, never looking back.
Each stop's a surprise, full of fun and delight,
As I skip through my timeline into the night.

So here's to the paths that twist and divide,
With laughter as fuel, I'll continue this ride.
Not stuck on the map, but making my way,
In this theme park of life, I'm here for the play.

Ascent from Shadows to Light

Stumbled through shadows, tripped on a shoe,
With every misstep, I giggled anew.
The sun poked through clouds, a game of peek-a-boo,
As I danced with the awkwardness, yes, that's my cue!

Climbing uphill with a grin on my face,
Where the clouds laughed at my slow, waddling pace.
With each little slip, I learned to embrace,
The art of stumbling with style and grace.

The light isn't perfect; it flickers and sways,
But humor's the guide on these puzzling days.
I laugh at the blunders, the flights, and the falls,
For shadows can't stick where the fun always calls.

So here's to ascents, so crooked and bright,
To the playful missteps that sparkle with light.
With each little giggle, my spirit takes flight,
In this whimsical journey, everything feels right.

The Echo Chamber of Growth and Change

In a room full of echoes, my thoughts bounce around,
With funny reflections, I'm joyfully crowned.
Every quirk is repeated, life's laughter a song,
As I roll with the rhythms, I truly belong.

Meeting my past in a comical spree,
It's a party of memories — just wait till you see!
With voices all jumbled, the past and the now,
I giggle at ghosts that still take a bow.

A riddle of growth echoing loud through the air,
With each silly trip, I toss up my hair.
Like a hall of misfits, we gather in cheer,
Celebrating change with a grin and a beer.

So here's to the echoes that crazily ring,
In this grand little sanctuary where we laugh and sing.
For growth isn't tidy and change has its flair,
But through funny reflections, we dance without care.

Scribbles in the Sands of Eternity

With a stick I draw my dreams,
The tide comes in, or so it seems.
Each wave a laugh, each swirl a jest,
My castles crumble, but I love the mess.

I sketch my plans, as birds fly high,
Then trip on seaweed and say, oh my!
The ocean giggles, it knows my plight,
As I dance around in morning light.

Yet as the sun begins to dip,
I find a shell, give it a grip.
With every grain, a new chance blooms,
My scribbled thoughts fill up the rooms.

Life's just scribbles, a doodle spree,
With goofy sketches, it's plain to see.
Hold on to laughter, embrace the show,
In the sands of time, let joy overflow.

The Mosaic of Mistakes and Miracles

In pottery class, I shaped a vase,
It turned out lopsided, a funny face.
With colors ablaze, I call it art,
A miracle born from a clumsy start.

I spilled my coffee, watched it swirl,
A fragrant mess, a caffeine whirl.
Add a donut, oh what a sight,
Mistakes become treats, what a delight!

With every mishap, a lesson learned,
In life's grand quilt, each patch discerned.
Stitch my blunders, watch them blend,
In the mosaic's heart, laughter won't end.

So raise a glass to all that's missed,
To wiggles and wobbles, we can't resist.
In this silly dance, we find our tune,
A joyful rhythm beneath the moon.

Unraveling the Fabric of Thoughts

With thread and needle, I sew my mind,
A patchwork of wonder, so unrefined.
One loop for the giggles, another for sighs,
As I stitch together all the whys.

Thoughts tangled up, like a cat in yarn,
Purring confusion, no cause for alarm.
Each tangled knot, a story to tell,
Of fail and flail, oh how it fell!

As I pull a thread, what will I find?
Surprises await, a quirky kind.
In dreams of fabric, I laugh and weave,
With each silly thought, I trick and deceive.

So let's unravel the patterns we make,
The fabric of life, a beautiful flake.
Stitch it with humor, wear it with pride,
In this wacky garment, let's take a ride.

Footprints on the Path of Uncertainty

Step by step on this winding trail,
With mismatched shoes, I fear to fail.
Each footprint tells a clumsy tale,
Of laughs and stumbles, and times I flail.

A leap of faith or a hop and skip,
Sometimes I trip, but oh, I won't rip.
Each misstep a dance, a whimsical twist,
On the path of doubt, I surely exist.

Though the way may twist and turn,
My heart ignites with a playful burn.
So here's to the footprints, chaotic and bright,
In this silly journey, I find delight.

Whether lost in thoughts or lost in woods,
I'll laugh at the detours, in funny hoods.
So come take a stroll, let's laugh and play,
On this path of mishaps, we'll find our way.

Seeking the Unseen

I searched for wisdom in a shoe,
But all I found was a missing boo.
The fridge hums tales of lost snacks,
Life's just a plot with crooked tracks.

I tried to catch the sun one day,
But it slipped by in a golden ray.
I followed shadows, lost the race,
Chasing laughter in a busy space.

My cat gave sage advice at dawn,
'Just eat and sleep,' then she was gone.
So I took a nap, learned nothing new,
But woke with dreams of a rubber shoe.

I ponder much, yet laugh aloud,
Life's a circus, I'm the proud clown.
With each wrong turn and silly slip,
I'll dance my way, let laughter rip.

Sails of Transformation

I set my sail on a sea of cheese,
Hoping to find the hidden keys.
The wind was strong, but I was light,
Floating past jokes in every sight.

My compass points to donut shops,
Navigating through sugary pops.
Oh, the map is drawn in chocolate stains,
On this ship, nothing much remains.

I painted my sails with a giant grin,
Waves of giggles over the din.
My crew's a bunch of silly ducks,
With quacks of joy and a bit of luck.

We ride the tide of perfect chance,
In funny hats, we prance and dance.
Life's a voyage, we laugh and sing,
Searching for treasures laughter can bring.

Journey Through the Unfinished Canvas

With brush in hand, I paint my fate,
Splatters of joy, a color so great.
But wait! A cat stepped on my art,
Creating chaos, a brand new start.

The canvas whispers, 'Try, try again!'
I'll throw in some purple, maybe then.
Each stroke is messy, a splash of mirth,
Like juggling jellybeans—what a birth!

I painted clouds that look like pies,
With trails of laughter that reach the skies.
My palette's full of giggles brash,
Will my masterpiece be just a splash?

I'll frame it proud, this wobbly piece,
For in its flaws, I'm wrapped in peace.
A journey whole, yet far from fine,
In all its madness, this art is mine.

Echoes of a Dreaming Heart

In dreams, I ride a llama's back,
Through fields of marshmallows, a quirky track.
Every bounce is a burst of glee,
Spinning tales that make less sense to me.

My heart beats funny, with rhythm wild,
Like a dance-off between a cat and a child.
Each giggle echoes through spaces bright,
Making shadows take flight in the night.

Chasing starlight on my fuzzy toes,
I whisper secrets to petals and crows.
The universe chuckles at my silly part,
In a realm where laughter's the finest art.

As I wake, dreams fade like mist,
But echoes linger, impossible to resist.
With a wink and a smile, I start anew,
Painting my world with a colorful hue.

Parables of a Soul in Transit

A traveler lost in a maze,
With a map that shows yesterday's ways.
He grins at the signs that point him wrong,
Singing his own off-key song.

Mistakes lead him to sights quite absurd,
Like a goat in a tutu, that's quite unheard!
He chuckles and says, with a little flair,
"Life's just a stage, and I'm the odd bear!"

Each twist brings a laugh and a frown,
Wearing mismatched socks, but never a gown.
With every wrong turn, he finds new delight,
In the chaos that dances beneath the moonlight.

So raise a toast to the journey ahead,
Even if it's led by the slightly misled.
For laughter is gold, and oh, what a ride,
As he stumbles along, with zest and with pride.

Bridging the Known and the Unknown

Caught between comfort and strange new lands,
He builds a bridge with his own two hands.
With duct tape and dreams, he ventures afar,
Asking directions from a passing star.

The maps are two-sided, and printed in jest,
With legends that leave him quite vexed.
"Is this tree a landmark, or just my old friend?"
He laughs as he wanders, unsure where to end.

The known is quite cozy, like tea in a mug,
While the unknown is tangled—like a cat with a rug.
Yet each step he takes, with a grin on his face,
Is another fine spark in this curious race.

So here's to the gaps, the leaps and the bounds,
Where the laughter of life in strange places resounds.
For as he juggles chaos, adventures unfold,
The wisdom he seeks is just laughter retold.

Fables of the Half-Told Tale

Once upon a time in a land quite absurd,
Lived a chicken who dreamed of flying like a bird.
With feathers a-fluffing, he leaped from the ground,
But he never quite soared—oh, what a sound!

He told half of his story over a slice of pie,
About how he'd conquer the vast, azure sky.
Yet each flap was just wobbling with flair,
A fable of whimsy, with laughter to share.

His friends would all gather, eyes wide with surprise,
As he painted his dreams with curious lies.
"I once flew above clouds, and caught a bright star!"
They chuckled and cheered, thinking, "He's gone far!"

In this world of enchantment and tales yet to spin,
It's the humor we find that lets the joy in.
For every half-told tale leads us to grin,
And the laughter of life lets the adventure begin.

Breath of Ambition: An Ongoing Saga

With a wink and a shimmy, ambition does dance,
In a peculiar waltz, full of misfit romance.
He dreams of the peaks, but the valleys entice,
Chasing after cookies while counting his dice.

On a treadmill of hopes, he jogs with some flair,
Spinning his wheels without going anywhere.
"Is this progress or just a bizarre show?"
He laughs while he twirls, saying, "Onwards we go!"

Each goal that he sets is a humorous quest,
With sticky notes plastered—ambition's best dressed.
Yet in every misstep, there's giggles to find,
As he dashes through chaos, with joy intertwined.

So here's to the journey, with its ups and its downs,
Where ambition winks back, sporting silly crowns.
For every sweet breath swells the hope full of cheer,
And laughter, dear friend, is what keeps us all here.

The Art of Becoming

I tried to be a master chef,
But burnt my toast and lost my heft.
I painted dreams with colors bright,
Yet they looked better in the night.

I swore that yoga was my fate,
But tripped on mats and felt the weight.
I danced in circles, thought I'd fly,
But landed flat, oh my, oh my!

Each step I take, a twist of fate,
I laugh aloud, I can't be late.
To find the joys in silly mess,
Is truly life's sweet, happy quest.

So here's to us, the champs of blunders,
Embracing laughs and joyful wonders.
For in the chaos, we will find,
A masterpiece, hand-drawn, unlined.

A Dance with Destiny

I waltzed with fate on wobbly feet,
In mismatched shoes, oh what a treat!
She laughed and twirled, then pulled away,
I stumbled, but hey, it's just ballet!

The music played, a jolly tune,
I tried to spin, but hit the moon.
She winked at me, quite out of breath,
"Let's cha-cha now, avoid the death!"

With every step, we tell a joke,
In this fine dance, no need to choke.
So step aside, let chaos reign,
In this wild jig, we'll go insane!

I raised a glass to friends who whirl,
Through life's absurd and messy swirl.
For in the clumsiness, we find,
A joyful dance, forever unconfined.

Navigating the Unknown

Maps are useless, where to go?
I did a flip and tripped, you know.
With compass stuck on 'pizza hut',
I laughed so hard, fell in a rut.

I followed signs to a grand parade,
But ended up in a wild charade.
With clowns and laughter all around,
In folly's joy, my heart was found.

Every turn's a brand new quest,
Adventures bloom, I take the rest.
Through tangled paths and silly schemes,
The unknown sings, and so it seems!

So here's to trails we cannot plot,
To randomness, we give a shot.
With laughs and joy, we roam and roam,
In the unknown, we find our home!

Labyrinth of Growth

In a maze of choices, I'm not alone,
Got lost in thoughts that I had grown.
I took a left, then a right for fun,
But ended up in a burger run!

Each twist and turn, a paradox,
Found wisdom wrapped in silly socks.
With hiccups loud and giggles bright,
I wove through trials, oh what a sight!

Life's a garden, weeds and bloom,
With rhymes and chimes that spell out 'gloom'.
Yet through the mess, I learn to see,
The humor in this tapestry.

So cherish laughter in growth's disguise,
With every blunder, joy will rise.
In the labyrinth's heart, we shall meet,
The comedy of life makes us complete!

Revelations Beneath the Surface

In the chaos, we trip and fall,
Chasing dreams, we miss the call.
Life's a dance we often fumble,
Laughing as we face the tumble.

Each new day, a game to play,
Searching for the light of day.
While we swim in ideas so vast,
We giggle at our clueless past.

Unraveling thoughts like tangled yarn,
Sprouting wisdom from the scorn.
In every blunder, laughter hides,
Like goofballs on life's wild rides.

Who knew progress came with a sprain?
With every setback, more to gain.
So toast to moments bright and silly,
In life's circus, no need to be frilly.

Seeds of Potential in Every Heartbeat

In the garden of dreams, we plant our seeds,
Watering hopes, pulling pesky weeds.
With each heartbeat, potential grows,
Who knew cucumbers could sport a nose?

Sprouting plans like popcorn kernels,
Popping up with all our journals.
Take a chance, let laughter reign,
Even chickens dance in the rain!

In every corner, a story blooms,
Unraveling mysteries in cluttered rooms.
With wild imaginations, we stumble and sway,
Getting lost in alleyways of play.

So shake those branches, let laughter fly,
Harvest joy as we reach for the sky.
With every heartbeat, let giggles ignite,
Because life's silly, and that feels so right!

Navigating the Labyrinth Within

In the maze of thoughts, we twist and turn,
Searching for answers, waiting to learn.
Each wrong way, a lesson screams,
With turns that lead to chocolate dreams.

Frantically dancing with doubts in tow,
Twirling and swirling, letting ideas flow.
A map made of laughter, joy, and snacks,
Navigating the mind, enjoying the cracks.

A detour here to meet a friend,
Stumble upon a glorious blend.
In this maze, we joke and jest,
Turning blunders into a fest.

So here's to wandering off the path,
Belly laughs and a brilliant math.
In the labyrinth, let's paint the walls,
With doodles and giggles, as adventure calls!

The Symphony of Unwritten Pages

In the book of life, the ink runs dry,
Every chapter filled with a sigh.
We pen our stories, with quirky flair,
Trying not to mess up our hair.

With each blank page, we boldly write,
Sometimes we giggle at our own fright.
In curious rhythms, our tales unfold,
Like socks mismatched, oh so bold!

Composing sonnets while we eat pie,
Hitting high notes as we ask why.
In this symphony, flutes drop their keys,
But who really minds when it's a tease?

So pen your story, let laughter hum,
In unwritten pages, we find the fun.
Embrace the chaos, dance on the stage,
For each flub is just wisdom's wage.

The Chronicles of Yesterday and Tomorrow

Yesterday I tripped on fate,
While tomorrow's lunch waits with debate.
I laughed at my socks, mismatched with glee,
Life's silly dance, oh come join me!

The past is like toast, sometimes burned,
Tomorrow's a puzzle, yet to be turned.
With giggles and snorts, we chart our course,
Life's a wild ride, a quirky force.

Memoirs of blunders and fun times we share,
Like forgetting my keys, or losing my hair.
As time spins around, we spin too,
In this game of chance, just me and you!

So let's grab a laugh, or two if we dare,
Collect silly moments, toss 'em in air.
For every misstep and unplanned delight,
Turns yesterday's shadow into tomorrow's light.

Synergy of Struggles and Strengths

Life's like a jigsaw, pieces that clash,
My strengths like confetti, my struggles, a bash.
Together they twirl, in a whirlwind dance,
A humorous mishap, a whimsical chance!

Some days I'm a hero, some days just a mime,
With blunders in rhythm, we all find our rhyme.
Laughter's the glue, it sticks all the cracks,
In the circus of chaos, we're all just on tracks.

I wrestle with worry, then chuckle aloud,
Almost forgot how to stand out in a crowd.
My strengths may be silly, my struggles quite dumb,
Yet together they sing, like a beat on a drum.

So here's to the chaos, to strength born from pies,
To sprinkles of joy that sparkle with size!
In the blend of our quirks, we find perfect cheer,
Together we flourish, year after year!

Paths Intertwined in Shared Experiences

In the web of our days, we stumble and weave,
Every shared moment, something to believe.
With coffee spills, laughter bubbles and flows,
Our stories together, who knows how it goes?

Two paths converge, like rivers that sing,
With tales of mishaps, we joyfully bring.
We trip on opinions, we dive into pies,
But together, we rise, like the sun in our eyes.

Shared secrets and laughs, like glittery trails,
Sailing through storms, on adventures that sail.
Finding joy in the chaos, embracing surprise,
As our journeys entwine beneath big open skies.

So let's toast to the way that our lives intertwine,
With goofy decisions that somehow align.
For life's only fun when we share all the quirks,
Creating a tale that endlessly works.

The Fire of Passion's Attainment

They say passion's a fire that burns bright and wild,
But sometimes it feels like just being a child.
As I chase down my dreams, in sneakers and haste,
I trip over laughter and my lunch—what a waste!

With each singed ambition, I learn more each day,
My heart's a wild beast, but my feet tend to sway.
Sparkles from blunders ignite the whole show,
Painting my journey with colors that glow.

So gather your humor, and let courage grow,
In the kitchen of life, sometimes spills overflow.
But amidst burnt edges and half-baked requests,
I find my sweet groove in these colorful quests.

With flames of delight sparking bright in my soul,
I twist and I turn, and I dance to my goal.
For every mishap brings wisdom anew,
A hilarious journey that's waiting for you!

Embracing Impermanence's Dance

We waltz through days with socks askew,
Juggling dreams while chasing a shoe.
Laughter erupts at the falls we take,
A comedy show in each misstep we make.

Life spins like a hula hoop, round and round,
Who knew tumbling could be so profound?
With each twist and turn, we find our beat,
A joyful jig with our two left feet.

A Tapestry of Trials and Triumphs

Sewing together our quirky threads,
Buttoned-up dreams and a few loose ends.
Stitching the moments, both bright and grim,
Our life's a tapestry, though ragged and slim.

Each mistake's a patch, oh look, a star!
Who knew failure could take us so far?
With laughter as needle, and joy as the yarn,
We weave a story that's light and warm.

Navigating the Uncharted Waters

A pirate's life? Oh what a vibe!
Searching for treasure, eating only bribe.
No compass needed, just a fun map,
We sail the seas, avoiding the trap.

Every wave's a giggle, every storm a jest,
Life's a big ocean, and we're just a pest.
Making waves with rubber ducky speed,
Navigating goofiness is all we need.

Reflections in the Mirror of Time

Looking in mirrors, what do we see?
A funhouse version of you and me!
Each wrinkle's a story, each smile a cheer,
Life's comedy club, and we're all the near.

Time's a prankster, it pulls all the tricks,
Turning grown-ups to kids, with its magic mix.
So let's raise a toast with our mugs of cheer,
To the laughter and love we hold most dear.

Steps in the Sand

With every step, a footprint made,
But then a wave comes, it's all betrayed.
Like building castles, oh what a sight,
Only to watch them vanish at night.

I'd change my path, but where to roam?
Each twist and turn feels like home.
With laughter as guide, I dance a jig,
At each new stumble, I feel quite big.

Fragments of a Broader Canvas

A brush of chaos, a splash of paint,
Is this a masterpiece, or more a faint?
I try to sketch with flair and style,
But often end up with scribbles and guile.

Each color blends in the wildest way,
Like mixing ketchup with my parfait.
Yet in this mess, I find my grin,
In every drop, new tales begin.

Echoes of Our Becoming

I shout my dreams into the void,
They bounce back loudly, quite overjoyed.
Each echo tells tales of past mistakes,
Like falling into lakes, or baking cakes.

But hey, what fun in tangled nets,
Catching hope while dodging regrets.
So let them ring, those silly sounds,
In this game of life, joy abounds.

Threads of Change

A stitch here, a patch there on the go,
Life's quilt is messy, a stylish show.
Each fabric speaks of laughs and cries,
Even the frayed bits wear their ties.

As I weave and pull, patterns will shift,
Who knew growing up felt like a gift?
In these threads, I find what binds,
A tapestry bright where humor finds.

The Canvas of Choices Yet to Paint

With brushes in hand and paint on my cheek,
I ponder the colors--they're all quite unique.
A splash of blue here, a twist of bright red,
Oh look, I've painted a dog in a sled!

Each choice is a stroke that feels so wacky,
Should I use polka dots or keep it tacky?
Mistakes are just doodles, or so they say,
In this artful chaos, I'll surely find play.

Some days I'm Picasso, some days I'm a fool,
Yet on this canvas, I make my own rule.
With laughter and joy, I hide the odd glares,
As paint splatters dance in the wild air.

Each layer I add brings a chuckle and cheer,
A masterpiece born from my whims and my sneers.
So here I embrace the mess that I've made,
In this colorful journey, I know I won't fade.

Breaths of Change in a Still Life

An apple sits plump on the table so fine,
But wait, it just sneezed--that's no regular sign!
A pear threw a party, with grapes all aglow,
And the basket just laughed, in a wholesome show.

Life's like this still life, with quirks all around,
A twist of the ordinary, fun can be found.
The snacks may get stale, but we start a new game,
As cookies start waltzing--oh, what a mad claim!

"Inhale," said the breadroll, "let's rise to the top!"
While salt shakers giggled, giving life a hard stop.
With laughter as seasoning, we're mixing it right,
In the kitchen of life, we stir through the night.

So breathe in the wild, taste the fun on your plate,
With each quirky breath, life seems pretty great.
A still life of laughter, with each twist and turn,
In this canvas of chaos, there's always a burn.

States of Transition: A Poet's Voyage

In search of some wisdom, I packed up my socks,
And sailed through the skies in a boat made of rocks.
With a rhyme for a sail and a pun for a mast,
I journeyed through waters that drifted me fast.

The waves were quite grumpy, they'd splash and they'd sputter,
"Is that a haiku?" one sea turtle did mutter.
But I tossed out a limerick, all done with a flair,
And soon we were laughing, with nary a care.

The ocean a playground, with fish in top hats,
Each line that I wrote, drew in curious chats.
With each splash and giggle, new verses unfurled,
In this quirky adventure, a whole new world.

So here on my boat made of phrases and dreams,
I float on the tide of my poetic schemes.
With laughter around me, I drift without fear,
For every misstep brings new joys very near.

Harmonies of Imperfect Moments

A symphony played on a spoon and a pot,
With drumsticks of bread, oh, sounds that hit the spot!
The cat joined the chorus with an off-key meow,
In this funny rhapsody, we're making it now.

The blender revved up, in a mad dance of glee,
While the fridge hummed along, oh, so out of key!
Each note a sweet blunder, each beat a delight,
Together we waltz through the chaotic night.

So here's to the fumbles, the slips and the slides,
To harmonies woven where laughter abides.
With every misstep, a new song is born,
In this mismatched ensemble, we weather the storm.

So raise up your spoons, let the laughter resound,
Embrace every clang, each harmonious sound.
In this silly concert where mistakes intertwine,
We find that perfection is merely a line.

Questions at Dawn

Why do toasters always burn?
And socks disappear, not return?
Do cats judge us with their gaze?
Or is it just a sleepy phase?

Is cereal soup? Should I ask?
Why do we all wear such a mask?
Do coffee cups hold secret lore?
Or are they just a mug's allure?

Do clouds have feelings? Do they cry?
What makes spaghetti do the fly?
Why can't fish come when I call?
Are my plants plotting my downfall?

At dawn we ponder, giggle, sigh,
With questions flying through the sky.
In the chaos of morning's light,
We laugh at life, it feels just right.

The Endless Palette

Life's colors swirl like spilled paint,
A canvas blank, but never faint.
With brushes weird, we start to sketch,
A masterpiece that's far from fetch.

The reds are wild, the blues are calm,
While yellows bounce, a happy psalm.
Each stroke a giggle, each line a grin,
What's messy now, it's where we begin.

Green's for envy, well, maybe not,
Just a playful splash or a tricky plot.
With every hue, we take a crack,
In this art show, there's no going back.

So let's mix colors, throw in a dash,
Make our own fun in a vibrant splash.
For life's an art, both wild and free,
An endless palette of you and me.

The Weight of Unsaid Words

I think of things I never said,
Like 'You forgot to take your bread!?'
The heavy thoughts just drag along,
Like lyrics to a missing song.

In crowded rooms, we play it cool,
While thoughts dance like a silly fool.
Did I mention that I love cake?
Or that my neighbor's bird's a flake?

Each unsaid word a paper weight,
As we all smile, it feels like fate.
Like secret wishes on a kite,
Floating far, into the night.

So let's shout loud, embrace each cheer,
And laugh at all the things we fear.
With weightless words, we'll rise and soar,
And share our giggles evermore.

Chasing Shadows and Light

Chasing shadows, I trip and fall,
To giggles and grins, I answer the call.
The sun's playing tag with my toes,
While I dodge puddles, where water flows.

Light dances bright on my silly face,
While shadows lurk, just a sneaky chase.
The trees whisper jokes, and I laugh along,
In a world where nothing feels quite wrong.

Around the bend, I chase the slide,
And leap like a frog, arms open wide.
In this dance of day and dusky night,
We twirl with joy, in pure delight.

Chasing giggles until day's end,
With shadows as partners, let's just pretend.
Life's a game, so let's play it right,
In this beautiful chaos of shadow and light.

www.ingramcontent.com/pod-product-compliance
Lightning Source LLC
Chambersburg PA
CBHW071852160426
43209CB00003B/526